WHAT'S IT LIKE TO BE OLD?

poems by

John Maynard

Finishing Line Press
Georgetown, Kentucky

WHAT'S IT LIKE TO BE OLD?

Copyright © 2026 by John Maynard
ISBN 979-8-89990-352-6 First Edition
All rights reserved under International and Pan-American Copyright Conventions. No part of this book may be reproduced in any manner whatsoever without written permission from the publisher, except in the case of brief quotations embodied in critical articles and reviews.

Publisher: Leah Huete de Maines
Editor: Christen Kincaid
Cover Art: Joan Arkin
Author Photo: Joan Arkin
Cover Design: Elizabeth Maines McCleavy

Order online: www.finishinglinepress.com
also available on amazon.com

Author inquiries and mail orders:
Finishing Line Press
PO Box 1626
Georgetown, Kentucky 40324
USA

Contents

I. Consider Old Age

1. Oncoming.. 1
2. What's It Like To Be Old?.. 2
3. No Reason To Ask... 3
4. Old People in Movies.. 4

II. Seniors And Senior Attitudes

5. Album of the Aged.. 7
6. The Heroic... 8
7. Two Oldies Chilling... 9
8. Crisis of Confidence... 10
9. Disgruntlement.. 11
10. A Little Off: Birthday Declaration... 12
11. Old Men... 13
12. Jump-Shot Air Ball.. 15

III. Diversions/Escapes

13. Moderate Adventure.. 19
14. Keeping Up, Keeping Up, Keeping Up.................................... 20
15. The Old Person's Elixir.. 22
16. Sex Young and Old.. 23
17. Dirty Old Men.. 24
18. A Retiree Dreams.. 25
19. Virile Dreams... 26
20. Regrets... 27
21. A Pensioner's Penchant... 28
22. Still To Live.. 29
23. Plastics... 30
24. Insouciance in Age.. 31
25. Considering Healthy Living.. 32

IV. Evaporating Immortality

26. Year After Year.. 35
27. Growing Mortal... 36
28. Longevity I... 38
29. Heartfelt... 39
30. Metonymically Speaking.. 40

31. False Alarms... 41
32. Fucking Pills (Complaint in Age)... 42
33. Losing Battle... 43

V. Limits

34. A Work in Progress... 47
35. Story of a Boy... 49
36. Compressed Morbidity.. 50
37. Mortal Muffins.. 52
38. Alzheimer's Happy New Year.. 53
39. In Here... 54
40. Waste... 55

VI. Ripeness

41. Lasts.. 59
42. Variations on a Theme by Yeats.. 60
43. Old Glory... 61
44. Time To.. 62
45. Eyes.. 63
46. Slipping Away... 64
47. Pain.. 65
48. A Sudden Jumping Joy.. 66
49. Old People and Ice Cream... 67
50. Aging: Against Vacillation.. 68
51. Youth and Age... 69
52. Invasion/Evasion... 70
53. Elms Bend, Oaks Break... 71
54. Good Days and Bad... 72
55. Rejuvenations.. 73
56. Illogic... 74
57. Reason To Be Alive.. 76
58. Renewals.. 77
59. Longevity II... 78

I. CONSIDER OLD AGE

Oncoming

I think I erected
These many poems as a fence
Against my own mortality—
Pangs and aches, premonitions
Of worse and worst coming on.

What were a few imperfect
Jottings to events that massive,
Looming to end all my efforts?

No consolation in the future.
That's sure. But exercise,
That's good in age. And so
I run a bit and let the lines
Run on in poetry—poems
That can stop no oncoming storm,
No sea. It will come on.

Verses thus written:
But perhaps
They can reach out,
Reach out a bit,
To those who might
Take comfort, knowing
They are not alone
Facing brute age.

What's It Like To Be Old?

When I was a young one
In my bright green
I thought many times,
Seeing old people in the streets
Of that little mill town,
What's it like to be they
Or even right to it, to my point,
What's it like to be old?
What's it like to be old?
Are they even like me?
Do they suffer all the time—
Seeing in town some who creaked and cranked
About? As did my Nana only once or twice,
Setting it away as on a shelf
Of hers, as she might me
When I enquired about her age too pushily.

And now I'm sorry I did:
She would have told it
Straight, the daily aging down,
The illnesses at times,
The delight of walking out
All herself, as good as new
If not as far, that joy
And the slow—or rapid—
Descent into dark:
On and off, restored, failing:
Like lights flashing, the not me, me
Still—here, me!

No Reason To Ask

People never ask
What's it like growing old?
How do you feel?
Does it change year by year?
They seem to think
It has nothing to do with them.
They have a special permit
And will not have to face
Those questions.

Old People in Movies

When they make movies
About old people
(And let's face it
They don't make movies
About old people)
Someone has to die.
No one gives a reason why.
It's simply in the script:
They have to die.
He's come through the travails
Of his later life, maybe a hero.
Good, then he'll have to die.
The couple who have found love
At last—deserved all their lives—
He's got strong feelings
Around the heart;
She's beginning to cough.
No happily thereafter at these ages.
And if they love looking
At the sunset,
You can see that's not just
"Beautiful"; it's an image
Of the oncoming night.
Let them try as hard
As they might
There's no beating
An inexorable plight:
The writer's and director's image
Of old age.
Maybe they're kids
Hoping for the inevitable inheritance
That stays away so long.
Maybe they never liked
That old producer
Whose wrinkled ass they had to kiss.
They'll give those senior movie citizens
Lots of caring sentiment . . .
And murder in the cameraman's eye.
Lucky if they don't get dropped hard
On the cutting room floor!

II. SENIORS AND SENIOR ATTITUDES

Album of the Aged

Fine old gentleman
Helping world's ill
Funny old coot
Forgetting his pill
Loving old lady
Taking a hand
With the tots
Sweet white-haired old boy
Sipping his ale
And telling his tale
A crotchety pain
Still dreaming of gain
An anxious creature
She's twisted in knots
A bon vivant old child besot
By the joys of the world
Through which he has twirled
A sweet dear old thing
Still thinks she can sing
Delightful patient
Entertaining his friends
In his room
An old sour puss
Just a silly old goose
A poor old bum
Calling for mom
In the gloom
An irascible corpse
Still kicking with life
An inert stiff
In the graveyard
Deaf to all strife
They're all much the same
Lined up in urns
They're all much the same.

The Heroic

It's not the note to sound when you grow old—
The heroic.
No one cares or wants to care.
King Lear tried it out and gave it up;
The giving up was fine.
Die with your boots on or dump them off
And show your ragged socks:
It's all the same to them, the always
Unremarking young, but don't parade and stomp
Like Civil War Vets on Memorial Day.
And don't vaunt:
Good as ever, sound as a
Hollow cave: you aren't.
Your brain is less, your stature is diminished,
Even your weight perhaps is down.
Don't clap spirit hands and sing. You might fall off
What little perch is left.
Think of Cheney working evil in the back room
Of the world's command, keeping "in there,"
Just as good as ever was: he wasn't.
And the world's worse.
Those eyes may glitter but aren't gay—
They're sullen and half dead.
Do not go bombastic into that great night
And don't bomb either.
The ill-doing, self-hating, fifty-year old
Is father to that out-of-season man—
Old Stalin at his phone,
The partner bullying the associates to the end.
The prof. upholding standards to the end.
The CEO still stealing salary and options
To the end.
Oh give it up, resign yourself to end yourself
As just yourself—
If you can find that just yourself
You left behind so many years ago.
Be a dear, and bud, bloom, blow
As you care to, without the
Blow hard; and skip the tragic thrill.

Two Oldies Chilling

Here we are
Watching ourselves grow old
Me on my couch
She on her chaise—
As befits that sceptered queen
Of past renown—
Doing no harm
And certainly no good,
Biding our time
Watching our time go by.
The dying young
Don't know the slow death
Of history passing by—
Not a tragic ending
On the front of destiny, winds
Blowing through flowing hair.
Not us extracted
But the world slowly vanishing—
All that we knew
Stolen away
And we still passing along—
Our world, dying, dead and gone
Before us.

Crisis of Confidence

Here is a perfect situation,
A café in a fine public park,
Inexpensive coffee, and good conversation.
Retirement paradise and they came there
Every morning and shot the shit
And reflected on just about everything—
Better times, lesser life today,
Careers done well, obstacles overcome.
There was just one adder in this
Paradise: sometimes it rained.
And they tried to tough it out.
Or some wouldn't come out at all
And their cowardice would be duly
Noted by those who made it and were
Suffering. Snow, cold they could handle
But rain was miserable and their genial
Outlook in their maturity came
To nothing but sog and sadness
And much talk about when it began,
How many inches will fall, when will it end.
And generally conversation, if made,
Was mean and short. The glow of life
Well lived was in abeyance for a while.

Disgruntlement

Old, we become narcissistic,
Sometimes fat and tired,
Doing nothing, checking
The options page in the tabloid,
Hanging around off-track betting
Generally not betting much
Taking our chances now—
Winning some, losing some
Netting zero most days.
The bus that takes you
From Chinatown to Foxboro
Or Atlantic City, coming home
The same day, a little poorer
Not much tired out.
Hanging with friends
Telling the old tales again:
Nothing new when you've hit
A certain age. Calling the kids
Hearing what's up
In a bit of a mist:
Good things are happening
To ours but not to us.
At day's beginning
We set out to find work;
Now we get going whenever
We want. You deserve it.
But what do you get?
Fat, a little lazy,
Nothing much to do.
The golden years
Soon to end.

A Little Off: Birthday Declaration

I'm here to say
On this significant day
That I'm not as sharp
As I was.
Everything I think
Has a little fuzz.
Everything I do
Is a little askew.
Memories don't come
Quite right.
I have to fight
To bring them to light.
Sometimes I can't spell a word
Now isn't that absurd?
Sometimes I call my friend
But the numbers don't quite end.
Combinations spin through my brain
But I don't attain my aim.
It's much worse when I forget his name.
When I go to put on my glove
I screw up at the nub
With thumb and fingers above
And have to rotate the hub.
But there's some consolation
To all my consternation.
I can still do my laces
Without making funny faces.
Maybe my rhymes don't come quite true
But I can still manage the loo.

Old Men

I've got a pension plan,
401k, Social Security
And I've put some money away.
I get settled down,
Stick my old head in the sun
Even run away to the sun.
It may not be easy:
Day comes after day
But each day I don't have
To keep dull care away.
Lots of old people like me
In our comfortable world.
I have my good days
My bad days and it doesn't matter
Much. Sometimes I've got it;
Often lost my touch.

I think of the guy with the push cart
Out every day getting older.
He's illegal here and keeps
To himself; his wife's getting sicker.
Their kids try to help
But can't do very much.
They've got kids of their own
And no golden touch.
So he's out when the weather's so lovely
But mostly it stinks.
Some days pretzels are selling
Some days there's only mute yelling
Inside: please come buy
Oh God, please come buy!
I think of the tired-out farmer
Still hoping for rain every day.
Praying his rice paddies will hold out
Till harvest day. I think of old man
The hunter, out on the plains—
His tendons are stretched
Near to snapping, those thin muscles
Enwrapping his perilous arms—

He's running as fast as he can,
Knows his hope is to catch
Something before he fades out:
Give him one more day
To continue his life race
Without any stop, anytime,
Anywhere. Endless the pain
And the struggle until
He shall come to his end.

The worlds of old men.

Jump-Shot Air Ball

I lobbed it in,
Made a poop-bag
Jump-shot into
A dumpster belly,
Missed the shot
And half fell
On my half-ass,
Poop-bag on the grass.
Is this the way
It's going to be
Now I've turned
Seventy-three?
Will there be
Worse in store
When I turn
Seventy-four?
Will I learn
To behave
Before I jump
Into my grave?

III. DIVERSIONS/ESCAPES

Moderate Adventure

Moderate adventure
Is all that I'm looking for
At my time of life
Try a new restaurant
Hear a new song
Take a different path
In my morning walk
Make a friend or two
Chat with a pretty girl
Try a new recipe
Stay in a new hotel
Take a course
In midwifery
Take a plane
Somewhere I've never been
Live the different way
Those people live
Take all my money
And buy a trip
Around the moon—
Or beyond . . .

Keeping Up, Keeping Up, Keeping Up

The Problem:
Not keeping up. I'm pretty sure
I'm not keeping up.
Is it they're going faster?
Or am I slowing down?
Maybe it's just both together.
Got me a flip phone
(*Finally*, said my son)
So I thought I was doing
Pretty well, until they flashed
Their iPhones and their iPads
At me as if to say
Gramps, get a horse.
Not rude like that, though—
They haven't got time,
They're moving too fast
To be rude or pick a fight.
Just a simple, get thee
Behind since thou art
Behind and let us go
Our merry ways, ASAP.
I used to think
I was pretty good
At fixing things.
Looked inside a computer.
There was nothing there
To fix! So they're way
Ahead of me.
And if the car breaks down
There's no carburetor to mess
With. Now they've got
Computers and warnings
Not to touch
Nothing. Of course
The cars have gone
So far ahead they don't
Break down much.
But if they do
Hey buddy, screw you.

So How to Keep Up?
I've taken my stand
Against not keeping up
Closer home, in music
And in poetry. Gramps
As I may be, at least I know
The music's been and gone
From Beatles to the Rolling Stones,
From there to reggae and to punk
And off to hip hop
And the rappers. Now I'm into
Feedback loops and
Revitalizing and reciprocating
Repercussion, done
With a funny
Visionary beanie
On the head.
Gonna get me one
Of those Meta hats
And then I'll be
As far ahead
As anyone. I've got
Great ideas for music—
Repeating rhythms
To the nervous pulsing
In my brain.
And I've got a poetry
Machine that spits out
Words as fast as I
Can think. Random.
Then repeats, repeats,
Repeats, repeats.

Wait, please! I'm coming!

The Old Person's Elixir

A glass of wine is the old person's elixir
If she's got a problem it's sure to fix her.
And when a wise man strips her,
He gives her some wine and then licks her.
As for *your* aging body, if something afflicts 'er
A glass of wine is your best pick sir.
And for the spirit—when mortal longing pricks her—
Take a glass of champagne with a fine brandy mixer.

Sex Young and Old

Darling touch me, hold me
Please me again and again.
You know how to play me
So very well, like a violin
By a master soloist—
Stroking my body all over
Drawing out wonderful sounds
Of joy I've never heard before.

You've had your pleasure now.
So get your hands off
My ass so I can sleep.

Dirty Old Men

You'd see them in the park
Feeding the birds, sly bird glances
At the young flesh going by;
Or at the local porno place
Hat in hand, gliding in and out
Without our notice—though we saw
Them all. Then there was the porn shop
With the mysterious hole within the wall;
Then down on Delancey, early in the morning
Seen with big bills competing
With truckers and sharp salesmen
On a break before the job:
Not their crowd, but they were there
Among those bums—and the real bums
Looking for a hand out, not a hand job.
Did they recall the years of easy love,
Of girls who smiled at them,
Smelled so good between the legs,
Climbed on them and called them pretty names?
Wives now gone and other chances lost.
Who forgot to turn desire off?

A Retiree Dreams

Let's skip the long tedious process
Of the spring, the ups and downs,
The warms, the colds, the many days of rain,
The hopeful moments, and the desolation
As winter comes again. Let's leave that
All behind and take a plane
To somewhere there are perfect days
Already, summer in full force.
No need to wait around for the joy
Of happy life lived at its best.
Leave behind the waiting tedium and the rest
Somewhere where the good moments
Don't unfurl and furl again. Rather,
They stay. Camels walking stately, palm trees
Everywhere, perhaps here and there a banana bush.
It's not my way but why shouldn't I
Get away someday and follow summer
Wherever she reigns in full exfoliation—
Nothing putting off or holding back.
Life as I have wished it to be.

Virile Dreams

In my middle seventies
I have dreams of virile
Old age: Kant living to eighty,
Woken and answering Hume's
Negative apocalypse. Biblical patriarchs,
Roman *patres familias,* my father
In his nineties, as he dreamed,
Pushing on his business,
My neighbor at one hundred and one
Painting those window ledges—
Still at his game of small-time
Real estate. For new times, I
Providing still new directions,
Riding still the wave of life.
New ideas, new approaches,
New conceptions, balancing
On my aging board without
Crashing in the surf:
Dreams the old have as
The young. They do well
If they live some happy life
At all. The old lucky to see
The next day. Dreams to guide us,
Young and old, while we live,
But we old now live to dream.

Regrets

Two old men
Sitting around
Talking,
Talking about
The girls they had
And even more
The girls they didn't have,
The deals they closed
And even more
The deals that fell apart,
The big ones.
Their theme was celebration
They thought
But you could see
It was all about regret.
Always wanted more,
Couldn't get it,
Still wanted more.
Was it going to come
Their way
The end of the day?
What price would they
Have to pay for regrets?
Only the crucifixion
Of their imagination.

A Pensioner's Penchant

Too high spirits
Are getting me down.
I feel like some foolish
Kind of a clown.
Lord God
I'd better calm down.
Is it the weather?
Is it blood pressure?
Is it the force of life
Calling me back to the strife
Of long jilted aims?
What is the point of it?
Why should I fly and flit?
I'm near the end of it!
Why can't I live without dreams?

Still To Live

Talking of future plans
And how one day we'd go
To Saint-Mandé and explore
Every day the lovely paths
Of the Bois de Vincennes
And that place in Crete
Down by the water's edge
Where we found shards
Maybe four-thousand years old
And every day in Luxor to explore
A new tomb deep under the ground
Or would it be a year
Across the Tiber in a little half house
Covered with wisteria vines
Where we'd drink red wine by candle into the night.
And as we sat in winter's clime
And had such weird roving thoughts,
We looked into each other's eyes
And one of us said, you know
I think the truth is that our future is our past
And sudden fleeting glimpses gave us
Fresh ideas for lives still to live.

Plastics

There's a doctor family
In the longing city of New York
Named Easternworld.
Some call them the Mephistopheles
Or just the Drs. Magic.
They freeze your sagging chops,
Pull the loose skin from your face
And snip it off.
They have a thousand merry tricks
To drive the goblins of dull care, dull years
Away. Beneath their calmly professional
Touch the years flow backward
Off the ground and up the hill
Like leaves scattered
Up on the trees in a reverse running film.
No hectics; only healthy
Juicy moisturizing fronds,
Liquid, lubricating.
They'll leave you like a plastic angel
Bound in amber, all life poured
Around you, nowhere to make a
Home but in your past.
No need to try cryonics,
Or cry for what has been:
It all will be
For eternity.

Insouciance in Age

I'm swinging my arms
And even swinging my hips
With a certain insouciance
Product of the day the weather
My boots not pinching too tight.
What have I to fear in life?
I'm taking it in my stride
And my stride is pretty wide.
I'm on the go I'm on the road
Easy going's the faith I hold.

Considering Healthy Living

Felt great this morning
Don't know why
Maybe I do
OK drank less
Last night
Makes a difference
I guess
Weight loss too
Got some exercise
Yesterday
Get some more today
Hey I may live
A few more years
If I can keep this up
But can I?
And why should I?
Health is great
But maybe it's not
The most attractive thing.

IV. EVAPORATING IMMORTALITY

Year After Year

Year after year
He wrote about
His decrepit body
And his soon demise.
He grew fat
Upon that thought
And used to chuckle
At his long remit.
He said he could not find
That day, his day,
In any calendar.
Nothing pleased him
Like his own reprieve.
On a day, one day,
The day found him.

Growing Mortal

Tens (I really feel like millions)
Of stupid little problems
Are fucking up my life.
Where is that simple
Nonchalance of body
That I used to wear
Like a steel vest; it's
Shot through by a hundred
Leaden, dumb, uninteresting
Pains and threats—more
Threats than suffering.
How many years have passed
With that? or make it
Simple, how many
Now are left? When will
Mobility begin to fail?
Put away those long walks
Around the narrow streets
Or shooting around on bicycle.
I'll get me a walker
And shuffle on before I shuffle
Off; or how 'bout a power chair:
Look out you cyclistas, motoristas
Here he comes, steady as he goes
Before he goes.

        I've known some
Highly gentle folk who refused
To stay the course. In the
Vanguard, they went their way
Leaving old age for the sissy
Taunters and the affliction whipped.
Maybe leaving some space
Behind for the young or
Young at heart—and perhaps
Some property as well.
Will it be a
Boom or a whimper,

My boomer bunch? Fare forward
Into concatenating desuetude,
Crumbling immortality, and all
Life's multiplying ills.

Longevity I

My parents were such gentle folk
They died without a fuss—
Passing on life to us.
They never thought
To have it all
Or live a hundred years.
They'd had their
Good time at the ball.

We all want to live forever,
Our dancing never done.
Our life's an endless fierce endeavor
Our dance a graceless run.
Just to eke out another day
We seize the rhythm of life away.

Heartfelt

My old ticker
Is a real sticker-with-er
We're been up some hills
And down some valleys
Still the damn thing
Goes like clockwork
With just an occasional
Twinge or quirk
Sometimes I hear
A pit or a patter
And I say
Now what's the matter?
But it keeps on its persistent way
Marking the seconds of every day
I suppose it can't go on forever
And wisdom says never say never
But still it's beating merrily
And keeping time
Along with me
Along with me.

Metonymically Speaking

As I age
My brain
Walks with a cane
Using evermore
Equivalences
Or substitutions
And not able
To nail
More than two or three
Proper appellations
Quotidianly.
What's in a name?
Everything
If you can't think of it.

False Alarms

How many false alarms
Do you get in a life?
Your leg, it's killing you
But it's a muscle knot.
It gets better, you're okay.
The tightness around your heart—
It lasts a day or two.
But you burp a lot and it goes away.
The neck that cannot move
For a week and then slowly
It eases off. How many
False alarms until something real
Comes on? Cancer, heart attack
Alzheimer's, you know the rest.
You live a charmed life
Until the charm wears off.
And it's what you always
Thought it would be, after all.
You're inclined to put it all
Together before you go?
When's a good time to start?

Fucking Pills (Complaint in Age)

I forgot to take my fucking pills
Of all the world's worst ills
There's nothing worse
Than having to take
My fucking pills.

Losing Battle

It went round the table as it does,
Sporadic, episodic, some nonsense about
Biden's son, how Trump's family is so worse
Than that. It drilled down a bit
On exercise for oldsters.
Phyllis said she ran a lot
And did pilates for half an hour
Three times a week. The doctor
Did three miles with his little
Dog, who always seemed exhausted—
But arrived again alive the next day.
I ventured I did push-ups
But on a bed with feet on the floor—
And everyone agreed that was better
Than the strains of the workouts
When we were young. There were
Sports clubs, Equinox, other places,
Prices, how much for a trainer,
What's that like at our ages.
The thing is to keep yourself steady
At it, though someone confessed he'd head
For the gym and end up at the movies—
With a big tub of popcorn and a thirty-two
Ounce Coca Cola. And overall
How hard it was to keep it up.
And finally the veteran, PFC
In the army, but later NYPD captain,
Summed it up: it's a losing
Battle, but it's fun to try to win.
Talk moved on to other subjects—
The weather, where Nadia had been—which
Country house—how was Michele's dog,
Was *Sgt. Pepper* the best Beatles album.

V. LIMITS

A Work in Progress

Tests and more tests
And this or that
Is fixed up very well
Thank you doctor.
Modern medical science
Is really extraordinary
Isn't it?
Then comes a day
The doctor looks more grave.
Some things we can do here
But we can't save the whole part.
And alas, we haven't learned,
Yet, to replace it.
It's such a tricky place!
But you can still live
A meaningful life
At least for a good time.
It's pretty important but not,
Absolutely, a vital organ
Like the lungs or heart.
You'll still have your day
In the sun,
I think, for a while.
Perhaps there's time then
For us to find a cure.
We're working on it
Steadily and we've made some progress.
But nothing I can put you in
Right now.
Let's keep in touch
About this.
I'll certainly let you know
If I hear something.
No, you can do everything
You've always done,
Just a little moderation
In everything you do.
You walk away from her

Or him . . . stunned.
But isn't this what you expected
After all?
Modern medical science is wonderful
But a little imprecise
A little half-cooked at the edges,
A work in progress
And so are you.

Story of a Boy

The boy took the pill.
He did not want to take the pill.
He wore the cast upon his wrist.
He hated every moment of that cast.
He went beneath the healing knife,
The knife that hurt, that saved his life.
He grew and took more pills
That drove pneumonia from his chest.
The knife again, shoulder all askew,
He suffered what he did—to make it new.
The stomach probe, the cancer tech,
The snips of skin to halt, to check.
He had his side-gut new resewn—
His muscles were again his own.
And there were heart machines,
And liver cleans,
And ointment tubes,
Skin creams and lubes.
One day he said, enough
You've done enough.
I thank you, but I'm mortal stuff.
Enough.

They filled him with formaldehyde
And took him for a final ride.

Compressed Morbidity

It's a meaning like
Compressed good health.
You do your exercises
Every day. You run
A mile or two.
You lift weights.
Maybe you get on your bicycle.
You go downtown
And back.
You get good sleep.
You keep yourself
In perfect shape.
You're just as good
As ever you were
But you work on it
Harder and harder.
So perhaps sometimes
You're better than you
Might have been
Twenty years before.
It's a great feeling.
You're at your human
Peak. Not just good
For your old age.
You made it with the full
Force of yourself—
A good mind
And a good body.

And then one day
The compression loses
Air. The great spring
Untwirls. Undertaker's
Assistant says he used
To be in pretty good
Shape.

Some young man
May read this and say,
What a cynical old fart.
He wrote but had no heart.

I have no doubt it matters
How you play the game
But don't forget the end's the same.
Think of a late long
Season when leaves
All cling, until
First frost, when
They all descend
In one sudden end.

Mortal Muffins

He sits in the park every day
And quietly reads *People Magazine*
And thinks, it's been enough
To practice these thirty-five years.
Time for a rest. But the brain
Doesn't stop when he sees someone
Obese and silly. And he sees who's
Done some exercise before breakfast
And checks that off on the positive side,
Watches those big three-egg concoctions
Going down: negative, especially with bacon.
Seeing the pallor on one, that connotes
A short life, the blood vigor of another—
Maybe too strong a flow, too heavy
A pressure pushing from behind.
All this he sees, knowing no one
Lasts forever, knowing what he knows
Of beginnings and of ends
In the mortal way. I say to him
These muffins that my dog and I
Adore each day, probably
Not so good
From your point of view. And he says
Well, you split them, that's good.
Still very rich. How old is your dog?
I say six. So maybe ten more years.
That makes her sixteen and you'll
Be there. I said, maybe with a walker
Maybe she'll come along.
He didn't disagree and I know
He was being generous. The next day
I saw him with a chocolate muffin,
Enjoying himself. But he didn't share
That muffin with his dog.

Alzheimer's Happy New Year

Forget the old
Bring in the new
So we can forget that
Too.

In Here

Outside
They're there
They're talking about freedom; justice;
Love among the people
There is light and air

Here
Dankness
Mustiness
Darkness
Bats fly in and out
Nothing seems clear
What is known slips and changes
Certitudes are things of the past
There are no endings but dissolutions
Galaxies spin faster and faster
Billions of them
Out of control
We are little creatures on this tiny planet
Down in the murk
Soon in the muck

Forgive me dear ones
I cannot sustain
What once seemed easy
Our hope and joyful expectation

Waste

Everyone comes to a certain age
Where they smile to hear
That youth is wasted
On the young. But fewer
Come to know a harder truth,
That age is wasted on the old.
The fine degradations of their loss—
The subtle or blunt lapses
In their health, the decay
And eventual fall—all this
The aged take too much in their stride,
Just to be expected, not for sissies,
What alternative do we have?
Or dampened fires in their minds
Diminish too the pain and anger
At their humiliation over time.
The brain and sensibility itself
May be half gone. But let
A youngster or even middle-ager
Arrive at our diminish-
ment and that one will know
To scream out at the universal fate,
Cry and decry why we were sent
And why we suffer to the end.

VI. RIPENESS

Lasts

A friend wrote a story
About someone who was doing
Something that he loved—
For the last time.
That was touching.
And he thought about
Other lasts that might come
His way as he declined:
Last sunset, last wine,
Last vision of the faces
That he loved. That too was touching.
But only if you were old enough
Or sick enough to have come
To those thoughts before.
Then you would know such days
Would come, such hours,
Such instants. And you'd only
Be eased if you were awake enough
To know them and say a proper goodbye.

Variations on a Theme by Yeats

I sing the
Latent theme
Of life and art:
The aging body
And the living
Heart,
The failing body
And the crying
Heart.

I sing the
Hard theme
Of life and art:
The aged body
And the unaging
Heart,
The dying body
And the undead
Heart.

Old Glory

I looked up at the flag
So quiet, barely twirling
In the lightest breeze,
And I cried. I am
Surprised. I didn't know
I had it in me. Flags
I've seen being burned
And didn't mind. Flags
At half-mast for great
And foolish folk.
And I thought only
Of them, whether good or bad,
But nothing of the flag.
And now, for no reason,
I'm crying. Not much,
Just a tear or two—
Selfish tears perhaps—
About longevity,
My own, and that old flag's.
How can anything last
So long. And it's
Still going, I'm still
Going. I see it puff in the wind,
Slightly twisting
Catching some sunlight
Before the azure fades.
I'm crying just a little
As I watch it from below.

Time To

Time to breathe
Time to expand
Time to know
That our life is grand
Time to contract
Time to pull back
Time to feel
Our lives deflate
Time was early
Time is late.

Eyes

The inner eye sees what
The outer never knows
And never thinks to know:
The shoals of misapprehension
The pains of coming loss
The shatter that will make
The end of all. It sees
All that and never blinks
Or casts its look
Away. It needs no glasses
To see what's really there,
No focal point to view
What's what or find its way
Among the wilds. It sees
What it knows and knows
What it sees. And nothing
Real escapes its view. That's
Why the inner eye is dark
And often sad, the outer
Bright and clear and gay—
Like light blue sky.

Slipping Away

Turning the precious stone of life
Around and around, warming
A facet here or there with my hand,
Cooling another one or two in the breeze,
Touching and questioning each part,
Tapping, interrogating, wondering
What will hold, what will
Not last for long, what had
Worth, what gave no value
To the stone—how blemished
A side—thinking how long it will
Prevail, what biding time, what end,
Trying to polish and restore,
Feeling the stone slipping slowly surely away.

Pain

Surcease of pain is joy indeed
The only joy we really need.
When we've found how bad our life can be
We're happy merely to be free
From trauma and from agony.

That's not the wisdom you learned at school
But if life can't teach you, you're a fool.
So enjoy the times of moderation,
Times of cruel pain's short cessation.
Consider you've found happiness
If you're free of pain, more or less.

A Sudden Jumping Joy

As you get old,
As you and I,
My friend, are lucky
If we do, you'll suffer
Days of pain, days
Of large discomfort
And days when you think
Perhaps you've come
Right to the end.

And so you may conclude
That old people grow
Morose, but that's not
Mainly what they feel.
They feel a sudden
Jumping joy
When things go well.
They think, here now
I may have three years—
Three months—three days—
Of good life.
How happy then they are.

Old People and Ice Cream

When I was young
I saw immediately
That older people
Loved to eat ice cream.
At Nick and Doris's
Where we went for birch beer
There were quite a few
Of them sitting eating ice cream
Out of big glass bowls
Like they used to use
For ice cream, some with
Whipped cream too and once
Or twice a cherry and once
An actual banana split.
Oh how they went at it:
Tooth-free some of them
With senior gusto like children—
Like me I used to feel.
And later I would think
They are like kids again
And later still I ungenerously
Thought, because they don't
Get *it*, they eat ice cream
Instead, like licking at sex
Parts that they ceased to do.
But now it's later, I still
Make love but love
Ice cream too.

Aging: Against Vacillation

When the doctor says you're kind of getting on,
And remarks your skin is rather thin,
When your colleagues all
Look through you with a vacant stare,
Or seem surprised
That you're still there,
When even the dentist thinks
We'll leave that tooth alone,
And your oculist reflects
That there's no point in changing lenses,
When your dreams say your long dead spouse
Is waiting to meet you over there,
When you know the ice is getting really thin
And it seems the check-out should begin,
When you feel it's really time to get along
And you think you'll just be going,
Then I tell you, think again!

Think that even old flesh loves a sweet caress.
Think of purple mornings sipping coffee
By the broad lagoon.
Think of laughing babies' faces.
Think of your own mug in the mirror—
It's been with you all this time.
Think how easy it is to find a rhyme.
Think of puppies kicking up
And how you once were such a pup.
Think of wine as deep as death
And the pleasures of vermouth.
Think of all those gorgeous sweets
That please your aging tooth.
Think of calm cows grazing
Deep within a Constable.
And if none of that's enough,
Think of all the pleasure
In bragging: how your later life's been rough,
That you're really really tough,
That you're still the good old stuff.

Youth and Age

Excess of life
Makes strong thoughts,
Strong poems.
Failure of life,
Weak ideas
And shallow performances.
It's the same everywhere.
Young mathematicians reorganizing
The theorems of old ones on the wane,
The grand old actor
Who can't recall his lines—
A handsome youth pushing him from the stage.
That's the way life works:
Ups and downs,
Its crescents and its descents.

But strong lines are not all.
Strong workmen don't do all the work
And the old often perfect
It. The descending moon is still
Large and full
Before the new one puckers up.
Age has its quiet triumphs
To set beside those boisterous ones
Of youth.

Invasion/Evasion

Had lunch with an old friend.
Old indeed I see he is.
The invasion that began young
Mounts itself more strongly each year:
New lines in his face—his cheeks,
His forehead—the hand shaking
As he puts a fork in his mouth,
Clicking on his teeth.
And there's a funny little cough
That doesn't desert him. I see
He's shifting on his tired buttocks
Side to side. Tremor in his chin.
He excuses himself to take
A pee—more often than he should.
Brain's as sharp as always.
Good on politics and plays.
But he talks a lot
About his doctors:
The defense army seems to grow
Larger each time we meet.
Teeth are definitely a problem.
He wonders if he ought
To see someone about some
Work. I discourage it.
I've seen some bad jobs.
But the resistance still is on
And that pleases me.
I think, go for it
Fine old man, as he leaves
Again for the men's room.
Something wells up, a big choke
Half way up my throat.
It's a long invasion
And it never ends until
The fort is down. Nice
Of me, but I notice
A tremor in my hand
As I pick up my fork.

Elms Bend, Oaks Break

Elms bend, oaks break.
When the hurricane came
You saw the take:
There were oaks smashed,
Acorns all over the place,
Great strewn ruins
Of enormous tall trees.
But the elms all stood
Broad as before,
Calm, ready for more.
The stumper came;
The oaks were all gone.
The elms let their long dangling arms
Swing in the breeze.
The great oaks were lost
The elms were at ease.

Heart of oak, they say
But it's a heart too easy can break.
As I grow old
Let me sway with the elm
And the great oak forsake.

Good Days and Bad

My bright blue, cranberry tinged, raspberry
All over, heady hued summer
Sweater and I feel good.
I've smiled at people
From all over the world
And some smiled back
At me, as if in recognition
Life can be . . . excellent.
And I helped an Italian
Who wondered what was
Inside the croissant—*cornetto*
He said—and my language
Was just good enough
To help him out. The weather's
Getting better and I feel
This warmth moving inside of me
To my heart. No heart attack today.
It's going to be a very good day.
I have my good days and my bad.

Rejuvenations

A tired old man
Pitying himself tremendously
And earning interest from no one
Descended into the Métro.
An accordion was playing
To gain a euro or two.
He stopped and began to sway
And then he danced a little
And everything was changed.

A three-legged dog
Limping heavily along
Found the perfect stick
And was a puppy again:
Shaking that stick hard
And jumping in the air
As best he still could.

A horrid old salmon
Made it to the stream's
Top, the still pool, and spawned.
Then knew, nothing more to do.

The old grandparents, tired
And grumpy, went to bed
And complained to each other,
Then fell asleep. Along about midnight
They woke, made love and were happy.

Illogic

It was logical.
He couldn't feel better—
Seventy-two but still
In the game—
Running, working,
Right in the midst
Of life. So he had to feel
Worse. Any new way
Would be a way down—
And he found it.
First aches and pains,
Then diagnosis of serious C.
He did chemo with vigor
And good hope. What hair
He had left all came out
But that was just
Temporary. Very tired,
Sick, vomiting—
All for good end.
But they pushed his system
Too hard and then he had
A stroke.
And the way ahead
Was logical and clear.
The illogic began
When he began to feel
Strangely happy.
He could barely speak
Or control his drool.
Every day they'd take him
For a little wheel
Within the park
And the air seemed
Perfect and sun warm
Against his dying skin.
If it would rain
It was like a blessing
On his tender flesh.

No longer in the game,
Barely in the world,
He gloried in all he saw
And all that touched him
And was happy
For the life he had.

Reason To Be Alive

Slip your head down and relax.
Nurse is coming with some snacks.

Some happy days are yet to come
Maybe the orderly will massage your bum.

Dinner comes at five
Reason still to be alive.

Renewals

Renew, for me,
Heart, liver, kidneys, gallbladder,
Lungs, throat, knees,
All whatsoever.
Every seven years do it
For me.
Renew, you can, you *do*:
Make it *all* new
Nothing forget.

(You're perfect, my lover said,
Thoughtful, caring, fine.
Only don't change.)

New, not older new. New
Like an automobile:
New brakes, new engine, automatic
Gearbox, tires, radiator, fog lights,
Posh fabric seats, even directionals
And computer. Make it all new, like that!

No point in that,
The goddess speaks soft:
We need you new older
Each time until, overworked,
Desiccated, all parts now poorly rebuilt,
You fail, sink to nourish our ground
And let new new perfections emerge.

Longevity II

The gods gave me some longevity
With much hilarity.
I find myself still a guest
At their jocular feast.
They laugh, I laugh.

But I seek out and forage
In my vicinity
The nourishing grain:
A long-lasting life
Of the heart.

John Maynard is Professor of English Emeritus at NYU. He has published five non-fiction books, including three with Harvard and Cambridge, and many articles and has done a great deal of editing, including co-editing a journal with Cambridge for 26 years. He won the Thomas J. Wilson Prize of Harvard University Press for his biography of Robert Browning. He has written literary history and criticism, including a study of Charlotte Bronte and sexuality and a work on Victorian sexuality and religion. His latest study was on the theory of reading and readers. He was awarded a Guggenheim Fellowship and also a NEH Grant; recently he was given an Albert Nelson Marquis Lifetime Achievement Award by Marquis Who's Who. He is a member of PEN.

During most of his adult life, he wrote some poems and planned to write more. As he neared retirement, he found time to write many more poems. He has been editing them for book publications for the past four years. *What's It Like To Be old?* is the second of a number of books he has in hand. The first was a set of poems, *Armando and Maisie* (2025), about the improbable friendship between his dog and a homeless resident of Central Park. That book won the 2026 Book Excellence Award for Narrative Poetry from the Chrysalis BREW Project and also won a Gold Book Award in Poetry from Literary Titan Book Awards. Much of his poetry was written while exploring the park with his dog. The present volume of poems reflects on the diversity of his own and others' experiences of growing old.

www.ingramcontent.com/pod-product-compliance
Lightning Source LLC
Chambersburg PA
CBHW030055170426
43197CB00010B/1539